# The Lancashire Coastal Way

## and the Wyre Way

*Fleetwood and Knott End to Lancaster*

*by*

Ian and Krysia Brodie

Lancashire County Books, 1993

*The Lancashire Coastal Way and the Wyre Way*
by Ian and Krysia Brodie

Published by Lancashire County Books,
143 Corporation Street, Preston

Copyright © I. and K. Brodie, 1993

Typeset by Carnegie Publishing,
18 Maynard Street, Preston

Printed by T. Snape & Co., Preston

**ISBN 1-871236-20-7**

**All rights reserved**
No part of this publication may be reproduced, stored in a retrieval system, or transmitted in any form or by any means electronic, mechanical, photocopying, recording or otherwise, without the prior permission of the publisher.

# Contents

*Introduction* .................... 1

1. *The Wyre Way* ................ 5

2. *Fleetwood To Glasson Dock* .... 23

3. *Glasson Dock to Lancaster* ..... 43

4. *Lancaster* ................... 48

# Introduction

THIS booklet covers the first stage of the Lancashire Coastal Way to have been opened. Eventually the path will stretch from the county boundary, near Southport, to Silverdale, where it joins the Cumbria Coastal Way, which continues to the Scottish border. Also covered here is the Wyre Way – a walk around the estuary of the River Wyre from Fleetwood to Knott End, which, hopefully, will also be extended to cover more of this delightful river.

This first stretch of the Lancashire Coastal Way to be opened by Lancashire County Council goes from Knott End to Lancaster. The route of the Wyre Way estuary path from Fleetwood to Knott End, a feature that adds strongly to the coastal walk, has been developed by Wyre Borough Council. The alternative means of transport from Fleetwood to Knott End are the ferry (check in advance on its running) and a round-the-estuary bus service.

Fleetwood and Knott End can both be reached by bus from Blackpool, and Fleetwood, of course, has a tram connection with Blackpool. Lancaster is also easily accessible.

The route is described in three stages, one for the Wyre Way, one from Knott End to Glasson Dock and one from Glasson Dock to Lancaster. A separate chapter suggests an outline for a short tour of interesting sites within Lancaster.

Much work has been carried out on the footpath and several sections are suitable for wheelchairs. The Coastal Way is waymarked to help you follow the route. The standard colours are yellow arrows for public footpaths, blue for bridleways (which can be used by horses, cycles and walkers) and white arrows for concessionary paths. On the Wyre Estuary Path in particular, there are some sections which are vulnerable to flooding during very high tides. One section of the Lancashire Coastal Way – around Pilling – is closed for part of the year and an alternative route is described.

We do not live too far from this stretch of coast and we visit it at all times of the year. However, a real winter's day gives us an ideal opportunity to walk the coast and is especially good for bird watching. In summer there are tourists at Glasson Dock, but they are mostly weekend day-trippers. Otherwise you will find the coast very quiet.

Further sections of the Lancashire Coastal Way will be opened in coming years, and other booklets will cover these stretches. A guide to the Cumbria Coastal Way is also in preparation.

If you are coming to the area by train then you can reach Fleetwood from Blackpool by walking north along the promenade from the tower. This is also a sea defence wall which continues all the way to Fleetwood and is the likely route for a future extension of the Lancashire Coastal Way.

For walkers of the Wyre and Coastal Ways it is strongly advised that you carry the relevant Ordnance Survey maps. These include the Landranger 102 map (1:50 000 scale) of Preston and Blackpool and the Pathfinder sheets (1:25 000 scale) of Fleetwood, Garstang and of Galgate and Dolphinholme. Together, these cover almost all the route described in this booklet.

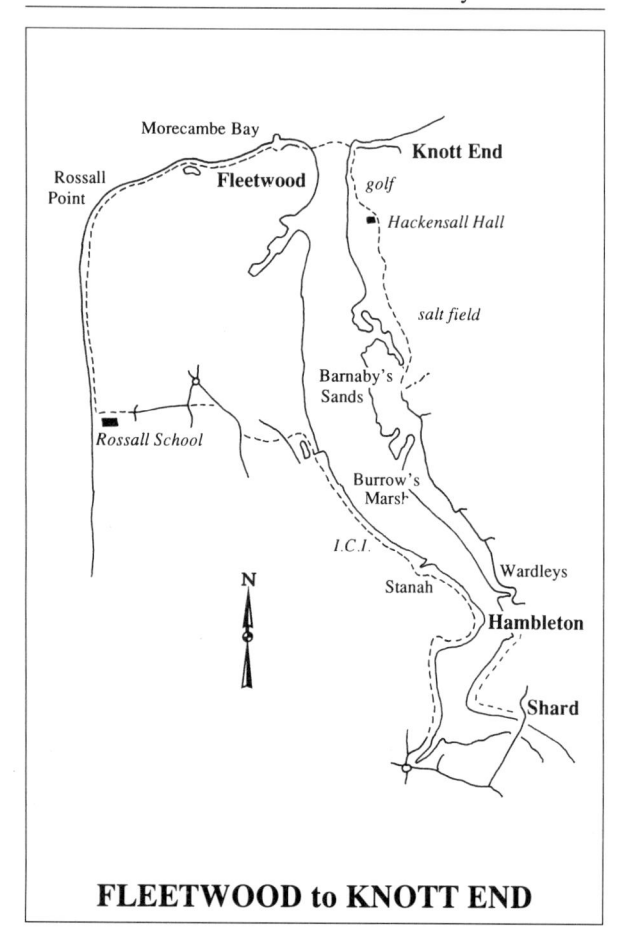

# The Lancashire Coastal Way

**FLEETWOOD to KNOTT END**

# 1

# The Wyre Way

Fleetwood to Knott End – around the estuary

THIS route, around the estuary of the River Wyre, has much to commend it – especially outside the summer months when there is much wildlife to see. Please note that some sections are impassable at very high tide. If you need to avoid such a path then an alternative route can be found from the relevant O.S. map. The mouth of the Wyre has since time immemorial been regarded as a safe or sheltered anchorage – this area may have been the harbour called *Portus Setantiorum* by the Romans. The estuary is unusual in that its actual mouth is narrower than the estuary further upstream. It is thought that, aeons ago, the actual mouth of the Wyre was at Larbreck, Blackpool.

The Wyre estuary is the mouth of the river that began its life in the Bowland Fells. It is a unique habitat where fresh water and brine intermingle at the various tidal states. At low tides it is an expanse of mudflats deposited by the slowing flow of the river, while at high tides it is a channel of water which ranges in

6 The Lancashire Coastal Way

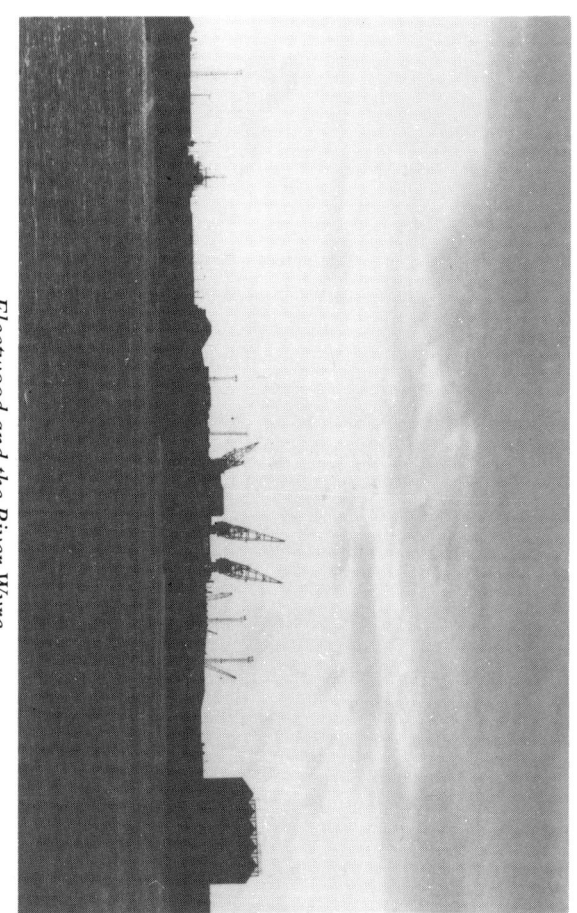

*Fleetwood and the River Wyre.*

width from 270 metres to nearly 1,100 metres. The adjacent saltmarshes are important for plant life and roosting birds whilst the mudflats provide rich food supplies for thousands of birds.

The river was used by ships until the nineteenth century when Sir Peter Hesketh built Fleetwood and its dock. Skippool was the main port for Poulton but Wardleys Creek also had its warehouse.

A Fleetwood perambulation can be found in Ken Emery's little book *Walking in Wyre*, published by Carnegie Publishing.

*From the ferry slipway, opposite the North Euston Hotel, go along the promenade, pass the RNLI station and shop, pass the lighthouse with the North Euston Hotel still to the left, and carry on to the diminutive pier still used by fishermen at high tide.*

*Just beyond the pier go right along the metal surface, follow the track and pass the beach bungalows and building complex to enter a more open area. We follow this promenade past the boating lakes, golf course and around Rossall Point, a superb bird watching location.*

*Continue along the sea defence wall until you reach two flag poles. Just after the second flag pole, complete with G 23 and its lifebuoy, go through the gap and down the gated ramp to the fence that separates the field from Rossall School. With the school on your right, walk down the fenced path until you reach the main A587 road, the last part being along a school drive.*

Three hundred years ago the coast was over half a mile further west than now. Erosion has taken its toll – hence the need for the massive fort-like sea-wall. The remains of a former forest are sometimes exposed off the coast at Rossall.

## Rossall

THE name is thought to derive from Rhos, the Celtic word for moor. The land around the school was owned by the Abbey of Dieulacres in Staffordshire until the dissolution, after which the reversion of the lease was purchased by the Fleetwood family. Ownership was then passed down through the Fleetwood-Heskeths until the land was given to Rossall School in 1844. Rossall Hall stood here, on the site of the present dining room, but a gazebo still remains from the days of the hall.

*Cross the A587 directly to go down the opposite B5409, cross the A585 and then continue along a track to the next road, which you should follow past the caravan sites to the right. After half a mile of caravan sites you will reach a terrace of cottages to the left. Turn immediately left onto the track after the cottages (before the ICI works). When you reach the edge of the caravan site go right onto the embankment path. Follow this path, which runs between old hawthorns, to a stile by the railway line.*

*Cross the stile, the railway line and the stile on the far side. The path now follows the left hand fence to the bank of the River Wyre. After crossing the road, turn right onto the river bank. Follow the estuary side track along the right hand fence of the ICI works.*

## ICI

THIS site was originally purchased by Fleetwood Salt Company from the local railway in 1889, in order to construct works for processing rock salt and brine from the Preesall saltfield (see later). (The brine is pumped under the River Wyre from the Preesall saltfield.) The company was acquired by United Alkali in 1890. The site originally had an ammonia-soda works and, in addition, salt was shipped out from Fleetwood.

Today the site, which covers 500 acres, produces chlorine from brine. This process also produces sodium hydroxide (caustic soda), hydrogen and hypochlorite (bleach). The chlorine is used as a basic raw material for plants on other parts of the site.

The range of products made includes hexachloroethane (used in smoke bombs and for degreasing aluminium); haloflex (for rust proofing, adhesives and paper coating); neorad (for coating optical fibres); polyvinyl chloride (PVC to you – for fabrics and wall paper); 'Fluon' – polytetrafluoroethylene or PTFE (for electrical insulation, low friction and non-stick surfaces) and victrex thermoplastics (used for their excellent thermal, mechanical and chemical resistance properties in the hi-tech markets).

*Continue along this road to the gate, where, on your left, the pipes temporarily disappear underground. Go to the estuary side track and continue along the final length of the fence to reach a stile, a bridged outflow and a further stile. Continue to the road after these and then turn left and follow the signposted path down to the marsh edge.*

## Wyre Estuary Country Park, Stanah – the Wyreside Ecology Centre

THIS area, now in the care of Wyre Borough Council, contains a car park and picnic site overlooking the estuary. In the 1960s the saltmarsh here was enclosed by an embankment and used as a council refuse tip. The area was reclaimed in the 1980s and a new visitor centre – the Wyreside Ecology Centre – was built in 1991. The centre contains a visitors' information point, an exhibition of the

# The Wyre Way

estuary's wildlife and heritage and a small shop selling publications, and there are also toilets and a baby changing facility.

**Parts of the path from here to Skippool and from Old Mains Road to Shard may be under water at very high tides.**

*From the country park take the surfaced riverside path upstream. After a few hundred yards is a picnic area which marks the site of 'Cockle Hall'.*

Nearby on the estuary was a small jetty from which one could hail the ferryman across at Wardleys. Alas, the service, like the old cottage, is no more. The small cottage, which once held a family of thirteen, was named after a great cockle bed that lay in the river. Its tenant called himself 'th'only squire this side o' th' Wyre'.

*Continue along the riverside path, round the sweep of the bay called Ramper Pool, and on to pass the moored yachts and boats. From below the yacht club building continue along the river and then take the access road that follows Skippool Creek to meet the road by Thornton Lodge Hotel.*

## Skippool

THE first record of this anchorage, now used by Blackpool and Fylde Yacht Club and as local council-owned moorings, was in 1330 when Edward III granted a road from Poulton that passed 'Skeppol'. The pool, through Main Dyke, drains Blackpool's famous nature reserve, Marton Mere. There was a port or landing stage here in the sixteenth and seventeenth centuries. Trade, as at Wardleys, was with Russia and included the import of wines, spirits, tea, tobacco, rum, sugar and timber. Guano (bird droppings) was imported from an African island for use as farm fertiliser. The customs house, first opened in 1708, was at Poulton.

As can be seen around the estuary, the invasive cord grass Spartina has taken over from traditional mud plants as it monopolises the available nutrients with its extensive rooting system.

*Go left along the road, then left again by the roundabout to cross Skippool Creek and its tributary, Main Dyke, before going left opposite the garage down Old Mains Lane. At the end there is a gate on your left just after the sewage works (due to close in the next few years). Through the gate go right in the field and back to the marsh and the Wyre. Go right along the marsh edge (it is very wet and rough and submerged at very high tides) to reach the Shard Toll Bridge by the toll house.*

The construction of a replacement Shard Bridge has begun. This may affect the route just upstream of the existing bridge. The new bridge will eventually replace the toll bridge and become the official route.

## Shard Bridge

SHARD Bridge is, at the time of writing, the lowest bridging point of the Wyre. Both the Shard and the next road bridge upstream are toll bridges. This structure is in the later stages of its life hence the need for a new bridge. It was built in 1864 on the site of Aldwath, one of the old fords over the Wyre. Shard itself is said to be from the Norse for shallow

*Cross the bridge on the pavement and after the stone wall on the far bank go down to the saltings at the edge of the river.*

**Please note that from here to Hambleton is impassable at very high tides.**

*Go right along the edge of the saltings. (Note the rocks from the Lake District in the boulder clay deposited here by retreating glaciers following the last ice age.) Follow the river around, go over a stile and, as you get towards Hambleton, go onto the embankment to avoid crossing a muddy creek. The saltings are notable,*

# The Lancashire Coastal Way

*Shard Bridge*

*unfortunately, for the accumulated flotsam and jetsam. When you reach Hambleton, continue on the shoreward side of the village and pick up the track that leads you to a road around Wardleys Creek and to the pub.*

## Wardleys Creek

LIKE Skippool, Wardleys was a port before the rise of Fleetwood. A small port with warehouses, it supplied raw materials to spinners in Kirkham. Some of the cargoes unloaded would be taken across to Skippool for transfer to Poulton. Ship repairing and building also took place here, and the largest ship launched was the 415-ton *Hope* in the 1830s.

The cotton and flax warehouse was demolished in 1972, and Wardleys is now a harbourage for small boats. Wardleys Cottage, originally *The Ship Inn*, was built in 1563.

The remains of the passenger ferry jetty to the Skippool side, whose service closed in the 1930s, can still be seen near the hotel.

*From here to Heads the Wyre Way continues along the narrow road, turning left at junctions and passing Burrow's Marsh.*

## Burrow's Marsh and Barnaby Sands SSSI

SIGNS state that these Sites of Special Scientific Interest are managed by the Lancashire Wildlife Trust (formerly Lancashire Trust for Nature Conservation) and Fylde Wildfowlers on land owned by ICI.

Both these ungrazed SSSI's are unique in Lancashire. Burrow's Marsh, especially, shows a wide range of saltmarsh zonation, including brackish marsh at the upper level. The SSSI's provide biologists with a natural habitat to compare with the more usual grazed saltmarshes. The lower reaches of the marsh have been colonized since the 1940s by cordgrass (*Spartina*), which spreads rapidly, particularly in estuaries carrying nitrate and phosphate loads from sewage works. Both sites are noted for the occurrence of common and flax-flowered sea lavender.

Furthermore, both marshes are of local importance for wader roosts and other wildfowl – hence the need to avoid disturbance at low tide.

*After Burrow's Marsh continue along the road to pass the houses and caravan sites at Heads. When the road ends, and a bridlepath follows the private road to the right, continue straight on to climb the embankment of Barnaby Sands saltmarsh.*

The small hillock at the northern end of the marsh is a glacial drumlin called Arm Hill which adds to the diversity of this SSSI. To the right can be seen the brine wells of Preesall saltfield.

## Preesall Saltfield

THE saltfield was discovered in 1872 during prospecting for iron ore. The bed of rock salt is about 400 feet (120m) thick and lies about 300 feet (90m) below the surface. It is said that prospectors took a sample back to their lodgings in Preesall which their landlady dissolved, filtered and boiled to produce the first sample of Preesall salt.

A mine was opened, but now the only method of extraction is the dissolving of salt to produce brine. The well heads used in this process form a distinctive feature of the landscape. Sufficient salt to leave pillars is left but in the early days subsidence, as the number of nearby surface ponds demonstrates, was a major problem.

Salt had earlier been obtained from the estuary by evaporation of salt water from the river in dry months. There are records of such an industry in Hambleton from the fifteenth century to around 1715.

*Go straight ahead along the embankment, ignoring the track which leads off to the right, and follow the embankment until it ends by a track just before two overhead wire poles.*

The track you cross here was, at the turn of the century, a railway from the saltmine to Preesall jetty, from which steamers of up to 1,200 tons would ship out the salt. Salt from jetties around the estuary ended up in Australia, South America, the Baltic, Canada, India, Burma, the Faroes and Iceland. It was renowned for its brilliant colour and flocculent nature.

*Continue straight ahead, passing to the immediate right of the poles, along a track that takes you through a gap in the hedge, past a small, wind-stunted wood and the lower end of the golf course to reach Hackensall Hall.*

## Hackensall Hall

HACKENSALL is thought to be derived from the name of a Viking – Hakon – who settled here in the ninth or early tenth century. Richard and Anne Fleetwood of Rossall built the hall in 1656 because Rossall was vulnerable to flooding by the sea. There may have been an earlier moated house on the site. The hall was considerably renovated during the nineteenth century by the then lord of the manor, Sir James Bourne. Tradition states that during this work two concealed skeletons were found in the walls. Some believe that the hall is haunted by a horse.

In 1926 there was a coin-find close by the farm buildings, which later became known as the Hackensall Hoard. The coins were hidden in a leather bag underneath a stone. Whilst the bag was originally found to contain around 500 Roman coins, only 339 now have their whereabouts known.

*The track meets another at the side of the hall. Turn left at the T-junction and pass behind the hall, but then turn right through a gate to the immediate right of the farm buildings. Continue along the buildings and then turn right at the next track junction which will take you to the golf course.*

*Cross the links, half left, towards a garage and electricity pole, go to the right of the garage and follow the left hand fence, with views across the estuary to Fleetwood. Continue down all the way to a house and cottage.*

*Walk to the right of these buildings and then immediately left to pass in front of them to reach the flood protection embankment. Turn right to reach the ferry slipway where you can rejoin the main coastal route.*

*Hackensall Hall*

## Knott End

THE large sandbank off Knott End is called Bernard's Wharf – reputedly after St Bernard. Many small birds, including knot and dunlin, feed here in the nutrient-rich mud. One story says Knott End derives from these birds, another that the Norse marked the channel of the Wyre with a chain of knots or cairns, the final one being the Knott End!

*Knott End and the River Wyre*

# 2

# Fleetwood to Glasson Dock

THERE are two routes from Fleetwood to Glasson Dock. You can either take the ferry to Knott End (or the bus if the ferry is not operating) from the landing stage by the lifeboat opposite the North Euston Hotel, or you can walk the Wyre Way estuary path as outlined in the first chapter.

The extensive saltmarsh and sand or mud flats seen from the Coastal Way are part of the Lune Estuary and Morecambe Bay Site of Special Scientific Interest and the Wyre–Lune Wildfowl Sanctuary.

The mussel beds off Knott End provide food for oystercatchers and turnstones whilst, at low tide, the mud-flats support large numbers of waders and shelducks. Along the saltmarshes around the River Cocker redshanks and curlews are more likely to be found.

The walk veers slightly away from the coast in the Cockerham Sands area and these fields are important high tide roosts for golden plover, lapwing and pink-footed geese. The freshwater pools across the embankment provide food for waders. You can also find wigeon and turnstone whilst red-breasted merganser can be seen fishing in the Lune. There are some important invertebrate sites but the flora are poorly represented. There are also nesting birds, such as ringed plovers, in the area.

From this brief outline it can be seen that the area is of most importance for birdlife, and as such is particularly dramatic in the winter and early summer.

## Knott End to Pilling

JUST above the landing stage in Knott End is the coastguard look-out post and behind that is a cafe which was once the terminus of the Garstang–Knott End railway, a line which was affectionately called the 'Pilling Pig'. A waymark post stands atop the jetty.

*From the top of the ferry slipway go up towards the Bourne Arms and then to the promenade side walkway. Just before the road on the right bends away from the coast you will find another cafe, one which sells very reasonably priced and wholesome food – the Country Kitchen cafe. From here to Fluke Hall at Pilling, the way follows the edge of the coast by going along the top of the sea-defence wall.*

Fleetwood to Glasson Dock 25

KNOTT END to PILLING and LANE ENDS.

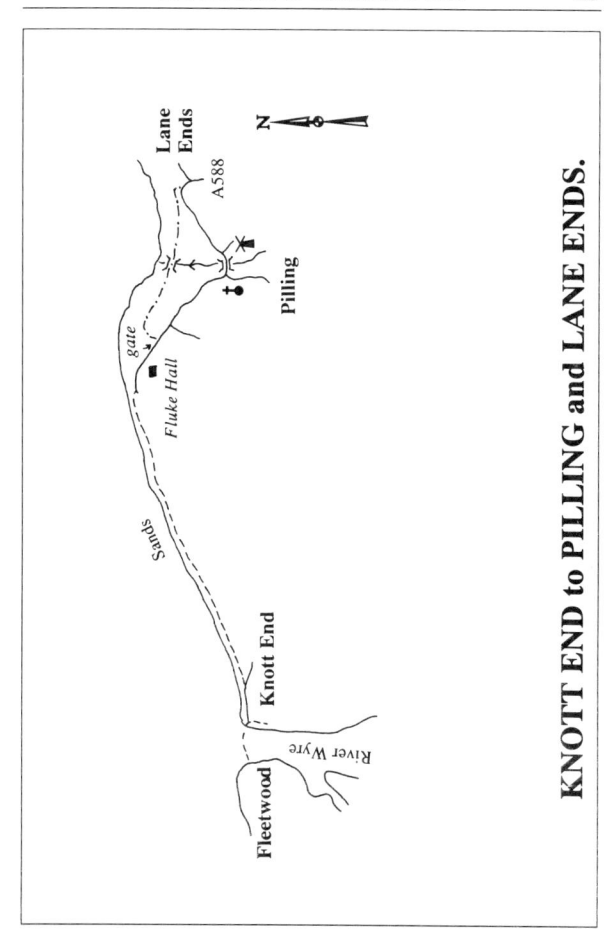

## The Lune Estuary Site of Special Scientific Interest

From the Wyre estuary, and almost into Lancaster, the route follows the edge of the Lune Estuary SSSI. This is part of the Morecambe Bay intertidal system and consists of extensive sand/silt flats with saltmarshes fringing the estuary. The estuary, together with Morecambe Bay SSSI, qualifies as an area of special protection through the European Council and as a site recognised under the Convention on Wetlands of International Importance especially as a waterfowl habitat (a 'Ramsar' site).

The Lune forms part of a major chain of west coast estuaries that are important for the roosting and feeding of migrating birds – this is why a small section of the way is closed during certain periods early in the year. Indeed, the estuary is said by English Nature to be of international importance for the passage and wintering of wildfowl.

In winter the huge numbers of birds are mostly oystercatcher, grey plover, turnstone, knot, pink-footed goose, curlew, redshank, bar-tailed godwit, pintail and dunlin, with some of these being counted in their thousands. Eider, cormorant, goldeneye, red-breasted merganser and huge lapwing roosts are also noted. In bird numbers this site ranks second only to the Wash in England and is the major British site for oystercatcher, curlew, turnstone and nearly so for redshank. The grazed salt marshes are noted for their transition from saline to freshwater conditions.

*When you meet the road at a small car park and access to the sands, leave the embankment and go down the road to pass Fluke Hall.*

Two gravestones were found on the seaward side of the embankment earlier this century. According to tradition, these were from the grave of a man and his wife who lived in a cottage near the shore and who died of the plague in the seventeenth century. It is thought that two sailors, who survived a shipwreck on the sands and were nursed by the cottagers, were the carriers of the disease.

This area of Pilling Marsh was once used to cultivate samphire.

## Fluke Hall

FLUKE HALL is an attractive stone-built property now used as a nursing home. Five fish in the stone carving over the door remind us that the name Fluke Hall is derived from the local name for a flatfish.

Around the turn of the century the house was notorious amongst locals for the goings-on of a group of theatrical people who met there at weekends.

The small house was extended by the addition of wings in 1902, and in 1924, the owner, the Lord Mayor of Liverpool, had the interior refurbished. Panelling, the stairway and a fireplace were taken from the famous liner Mauretania to embellish the house. Please respect the privacy of the house.

*Continue down the road, past the wood and pond on your left, and look for a gate, waymarker and stile on the left. From here to Lane Ends Amenity Area is a provisional path now under the auspices of the National Rivers Authority. Because the embankment used overlooks an important wildfowl area – particularly for winter visitors – the path is closed from December 26th to Good Friday each year. Dogs are not permitted on the embankment at any time.*

*During the open period, cross the field to the embankment, then turn right and walk along the embankment until the path climbs to its crest. Continue until, after crossing two stiles, you arrive at the car park at Lane Ends Amenity Area. The area is a public open space with facilities for parking and picnicking, and is a superb bird watching area, particularly in winter.*

*During the closed period you will have to walk through Pilling village via the road (a walk that can include a visit to the Golden Ball, Pilling Church or*

*Pilling Pottery) and on to Lane Ends Picnic Site.*

## Pilling

THE name Pilling is thought to be derived from the Celtic word for creek, but the coastal sea-defence embankment and the silting and canalising of the streams that flow into the bay hardly suggest that the name is appropriate any longer.

The church, whose spire is a landmark on the flat Fylde landscape, is named after St John the Baptist and dates from 1886-7. It was designed, like many local churches of that era, by Paley and Austin. Just south of the church is Pilling Old Church of 1717, with its box pews and three decker pulpit. The sundial over the door commemorates a former vicar, the Reverend George Holden, who first calculated the modern tide-tables.

*To continue from Lane Ends you must go down through the car park and leave by the access road. Whilst your map shows the embankment continuing in the direction of the route it is not open to public access.*

When the embankment was initially planned by North West Water, public access was promised, but, much to the chagrin of local ramblers, it never came. Hopefully, the situation may change, but the strong

30     The Lancashire Coastal Way

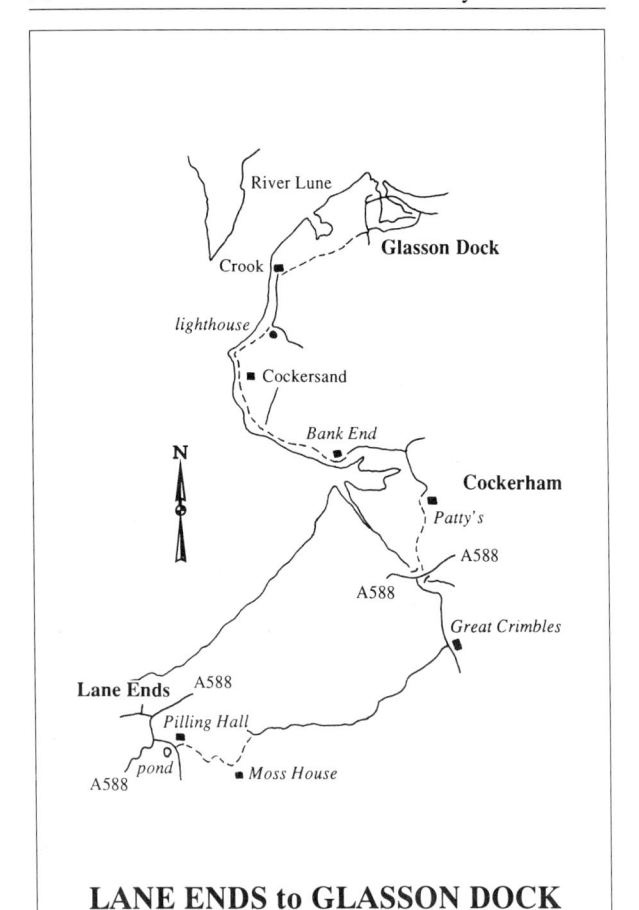

**LANE ENDS to GLASSON DOCK**

conservation lobby may continue to oppose public access on account of the area's wildlife value.

Cockerham Marsh was once used for cutting sea washed turf for lawns and bowling green construction.

*Turn left on the road outside the car park to reach the A588. Turn right here but take the first left turning, which is signposted Garstang and waymarked. Continue down this road until opposite the duck pond on your right is the entrance to the yard of Pilling Hall Farm. Again the path is waymarked.*

Just south of the farm lies a small moated site and some rubble – the remains of Pilling's first church. This dates at least from the early thirteenth century, possibly earlier, and was served by the monks of Cockersand Abbey, who farmed some land in Pilling. It was probably built on a previously pagan site.

*Turn left into the yard but take a sharp right to go down a concrete track before the brick outbuildings. Go through the gate at the end and cross the field and the stile by the gate in the far right hand corner. In the next field follow the right hand dyke straight ahead until your way is blocked by a dyke and fence. This is also waymarked.*

*Turn left here and go to cross the footbridge in the field's corner. This dyke being crossed is the boundary between Wyre Borough and Lancaster City Council areas. Turn right in the field and follow the right hand boundary through two fields, connected by a stile, to reach a track just short of Moss House Farm. Go left down the track and then right onto the raised moss road.*

## Winmarleigh Moss, Mosslands

JUST off the route and to the south lies Winmarleigh Moss which represents the last remaining uncultivated mossland in Lancashire. At one time the coastal fringe was well endowed with such natural features but land drainage and the needs of the farmers have led to the great majority of such areas being cultivated.

The remaining area is certainly wild and most of it is designated a Site of Special Scientific Interest. Another part is used by a farmer who gathers the peat to sell for home fires and no doubt for gardens – a practice now condemned by ecologists.

*Continue along this road for approximately two miles until turning left at the junction into Crimble Lane. This road leads you to the A588 where you turn right over the bridge and cross the road immediately to the left to reach a stile between a gate and bridlegate at the riverside.*

*Cross the stile and walk along the embankment top path, initially following the straight course of the River Cocker but later bending right to reach Patty's Farm. From here to Crook Farm the path is suitable for wheelchairs.*

## Parachute Centre

JUST behind the embankment beyond Patty's Farm is the parachute centre where, at weekends, a light plane can often be seen taking off to disgorge its load of parachutists. Some walkers may regard this as a bonus, others as noise pollution.

*Walk down the farm road, turning left at the junction, and continue to Bank End Farm. At times of very high tides this road is submerged, but on this stretch at least, the accompanying embankment can be used.*

*From the farm, take the shoreside path past the farm's caravan site and continue to pass the larger Cockerham Sands site. Follow the sites's access track along the shore to where the track bends right, becoming a public road, and your way lies along the shore edge. On the seaward side you come to an incline which, if climbed, leads to a path along the edge of a field, past a ruined wartime look-out post, and on to the ruins of Cockersand Abbey with its remaining chapter house.*

**The shore here reveals an outcrop of red permian sandstone. The next outcrop of rock on the coast is at Heysham to the north but you would have to travel to the Wirral peninsula to find the next southern outcrop.**

## Cockersand Abbey

ONLY the chapter house, of c.1230, and a few pieces of walling remain of this former Premonstratensian Abbey which was founded in 1190. Prior to this the hermit Hugh de Garth established a cell in c.1180 which, during the next four years, developed into a hospital for lepers under the patronage of Leicester Abbey.

The Premonstratensian Canons of Croxton, Leicester, took over the site to build their abbey, which they called St Mary of the Marsh. By the time of dissolution only Whalley and Furness had greater annual incomes among Lancashire's abbeys.

The ruins are the result of the dissolution and time. The chapter house remains because it became the burial vault of the Dalton family from nearby Thurnham Hall, who had the building crenellated. The last of the line to be buried here was Miss Elizabeth Dalton in 1861, who built some of the houses we shall shortly see in Glasson Dock. The fourteenth-century choir stalls from the abbey now form part of Lancaster Priory, while

*The Chapter House, Cockersand Abbey*

stonework from the building has been found in nearby Crook Farm and was also used in construction of the sea defence wall. The abbey itself was frequently threatenedby inundation.

It is thought that the canons erected the first light to guide ships in the Lune and held extensive fishing rights. Some ruins of an early fishing baulk can be seen in the estuary.

## The Lune Lights

THE Lune was a notorious channel for ships, even when guided by lights at Cockersand Abbey and Overton Church. The lighthouse by the channel on Plover Scar, and the one on the next house along the route, called Cockersand Light, were erected in the late 1840s after the port authority had been given permission to spend £2,000 on their construction.

*From the abbey take the path along the seaward edge which, after a further kissing gate, becomes a track and then arrives at a road junction by the former lighthouse.*

*At this junction continue along the Lune estuary with the hamlet of Sunderland on the far bank, to reach Crook Farm. From here the way becomes difficult to negotiate in a wheelchair.*

*The Lune Light*

Crook Farm and its shippon incorporate stone fragments from Cockersand Abbey, some of which are recognisable as former door frames and two-light window heads.

*On the nearside of the farm go right, walk down to the field and, after two consecutive gates, follow the line of old hedge. The track goes across a gated bridge and then follows a further line of hawthorns on the left to reach a gate. Beyond the gate the track becomes enclosed, passes the entrance to a caravan site and then meets a road junction. Go left along the road to the viewpoint indicator and then turn right to descend Tithebarn Hill to reach Glasson Dock.*

## Glasson Dock

UNTIL the middle of the eighteenth century there were few thatched cottages and farms in the area. Of these, Saltcotes and Glasson farms are still standing. Following problems with a rock bar, the silting of the tortuous Lune channel to Lancaster and the failure of the port of Sunderland just across the river, Glasson eventually became Lancaster's main port.

Following legislation in 1743 and the positioning of a large mooring stone in 1751, work began on the construction of a dock in 1783. It was opened in 1787 but with a quay on the east side only – the west side was just a sloping bank. Further work by the operators – the Port of Lancaster Commissioners – included the provision of a dry dock.

The three-acre dock basin once accommodated up to twenty-five vessels of up to 200 tons each, but today only a small number of ships use the port, trading in coal, animal foods, grain, timber and scrap metal where once coal, lime and stone formed the cargoes.

The land was originally owned by the Dalton family of Thurnham Hall, some of whom are buried at Cockersand whilst two are buried at Glasson Church. A dockside pub, the *Dalton Arms*, and a row of cottages built by the family are tangible reminders of their history.

The dock's prospects expanded in 1826 when the canal branch was constructed, linking the port with the Lancaster Canal and thus providing a direct route to the city. The canal company constructed a seventeen-acre basin next to the dock which is now an important mooring and repair point for many canal and sea-going leisure craft. It is interesting to note that the village was not planned but grew through the development of speculative terraces.

The canal lost its importance when a railway line was built from Lancaster in 1883, although this ceased to operate in the 1950s. A walk around the port and

*Glasson Dock*

village conservation area is described in *Field Excursions in North West England* (Cicerone Press) and in a booklet published by Thurnham Parish Council in 1987.

The village offers a selection of cafes, including one on a barge, and pubs. There is a bus service to Lancaster.

42 The Lancashire Coastal Way

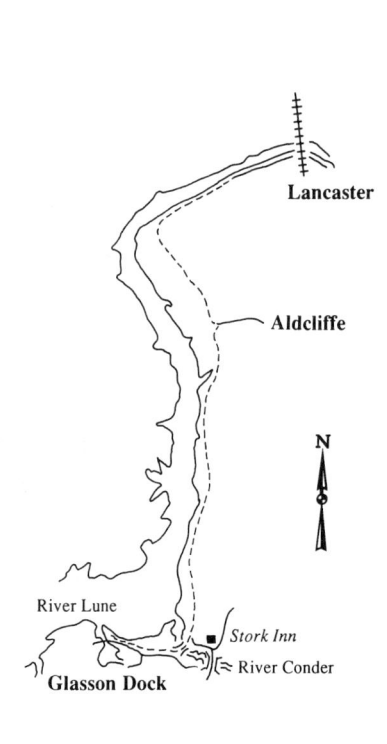

**GLASSON DOCK to LANCASTER**

# 3

# Glasson Dock to Lancaster

THE section from Glasson Dock to Aldcliffe has, like that from Bank House Farm to Abbey Lighthouse Cottage, been made suitable for wheelchairs.

*After leaving the dockside area continue towards the Caribou Hotel. Just to the right are some toilets and a bowling green; follow the estuary side path behind these. This path, for much of the way to Lancaster, used to be the trackbed of the former railway to the port.*

The narrow mud-banks and un-grazed saltmarsh of the Conder estuary often have small numbers of waders at low tide in winter and migration times. In summer, non-breeding bar-tailed godwits have been seen.

The poor soil of the railway line supports the best selection of wildflowers to be seen on this section of the coastal path.

The wide saltings of Aldcliffe Marsh are part of the Lune Estuary SSSI and are home to mute swans in winter. These are sometimes joined by whooper swans and pink-footed geese. Winter also brings curlew, mallard, shelduck and redshank, the last sometimes staying to breed. Goldeneye and goosander can be seen on the river in winter.

## The Glasson Branch Railway

THE railway was established in 1883 and carried passengers until 1930 and goods until the 1950s although it was 1962 before the track was raised. It was later acquired by Lancashire County Council for conversion to a path.

Its only claim to fame occurred in 1917 when King George V stayed overnight in the royal train at Glasson. Tales are also told of locomotive firemen who used to kick out lumps of coal as the engine passed fishermen's huts and, in return, there sometimes came a salmon in the other direction. On one occasion an engine driver was demoted after arriving at Lancaster without the coaches of his train.

*Go along the path by the left hand fence with views up the River Lune. Cross the old railway bridge over the River Conder and continue to Lancashire County Council's Conder Green Picnic Site where toilets are available. Picnic facilities for the physically disabled are provided. The saltmarsh by the Conder estuary is the home of common and lax-flowered sea-lavender due to*

# Glasson Dock to Lancaster

*Glasson Dock*

*the absence of grazing animals.*

*The railway path continues through the picnic site and car park and along near the river, passing under a smoke stained bridge by a house called Waterloo, a name that no doubt indicates the date of construction. Good views over the Lune can be seen along the next section of the path before it meets the end of a road below Aldcliffe. Below Ashton Hall, now a golf club, are the remains of the platform built for the hall's owner.*

*Leave the track at the waymarked end of the road, go left over a stile by the gate, and then turn right to follow the embankment path along the edge of the saltmarsh until the path eventually bends right as the river narrows.*

**On the opposite bank is Snatchem's Inn – a name which doubtless refers to the pressgang. The road by the pub is often cut off during high tides, as can be the next part of the path.**

*The path now follows the river bank closely all the way to the road, past some cottages, and on to reach St George's Quay. The road goes under the imposing west coast main line railway bridge – Carlisle Bridge – high over the Lune. On the future extension of the walk it will be possible to cross the adjacent footbridge to continue north. For now you must continue along the quay to the Maritime Museum and arrive in Lancaster.*

# 4

# Lancaster

ORIGINALLY based on a hilltop site overlooking the Lune, Lancaster has long been a strategically important town, occupied in turn by a Roman fort, an Anglo-Saxon monastery and a royal castle.

The town which grew around this hilltop has been a successful market centre since medieval times, gaining borough status in 1193 and city status on the morning of the coronation of George VI, the 14 May 1937.

Wealth came to the town with the development of the port, which encouraged trade with North America and the West Indies in the eighteenth century and contributed to the town's industrial development in the nineteenth. Today, the town is an educational centre, its university having been founded in 1964.

Modern Lancaster is dominated by its castle, the Priory Church and the Williamson Memorial, which can be said to represent the state, church and commerce respectively, each having laid the foundation for the development of the city. These three landmarks are visible for much of this last stretch of the Lancashire Coastal Way.

The castle and priory, with some odd Roman fragments, are all that remain of the early town, much of which was destroyed by the forays of the Scots during the border wars. However, the splendid Georgian buildings we see along with the open squares today retain much of the medieval street plan including some of the narrow alleyways that interlink the thoroughfares.

On our way along the Lune into Lancaster the first building of interest is the Kingfisher wall coverings factory which was once the site where Williamson, of Williamson's Memorial (see later), made his fortune from linoleum. Further along St George's Quay is the Maritime Museum.

## The Maritime Museum

Housed in the restored magnificent Palladian customs house of 1764, and built to a design by Richard Gillow, the museum portrays the maritime history of Lancaster and the Lune – some of which we have already seen at Glasson Dock.

The museum concentrates on the early eighteenth-century trade with the West Indies and North America, when mahogany, cotton, sugar and rum were imported and stored in nearby warehouses along the quay. Other displays include the life of Morecambe Bay and the story of the Lancaster Canal. A visit is recommended and will add to the appreciation of the coast covered during the walk.

The museum is open from 11.00am until 5.00pm in summer and from 2.00pm to 5.00pm from November to March. Telephone (0524) 64637.

*Whilst this section of the walk officially finishes at Skerton Bridge, just a little further upstream, people returning by public transport, or those who wish to see other places of interest in Lancaster will find the priory and castle the next nearest buildings of interest. Turn right off the quayside road just beyond the museum to climb the steep footpath to the priory, on the way passing close to the site of the Roman baths.*

## St Mary's Priory

MUCH of the history of this strategic hilltop site can be seen in the Priory Church. The church occupies the site of the Anglo-Saxon monastery which itself took the place of a Roman fort. In 1094 the monastery was a cell of the parent Benedictine monastery of Seez and remained as such for three centuries.

At the times of the wars with France in the early fifteenth century the monastery's lands were confiscated by Henry V and its monks replaced by a vicar and six assistant priests, thus establishing the parish church which remains today.

Notable features of the parish church include stones from the Roman fort (now in the choir), a Saxon doorway in the west wall and a font, also believed to be Saxon. The magnificent choir stalls carved from English oak are said to pre-date the early fourteenth century and are regarded as superb examples of the craftsmanship of their time. The majority of the church and tower is Georgian. Together with the castle, these buildings form Lancaster's distinctive skyline.

## Lancaster Castle

THE castle originated as a Norman motte and bailey soon after the conquest and was built by Roger de Poictou as a rectangular stone structure. It was enlarged in the thirteenth century, with the central Lungess Tower forming the nucleus of the current structure. The castle continued to play an important defensive role which is reflected by the addition of the magnificent twin towers of the gatehouse added by Henry IV. The gateway is named after Henry's father, John of Gaunt, whose full length statue can be seen over the arch.

The castle saw action during the border wars, the Civil War and the Jacobite rebellion and additionally, since 1166, has acted as a centre for the dispensation of

*Lancaster Castle.*

justice and punishment.

Many prisoners have languished in its dungeons and many have left by cart for execution on Lancaster Moor. Catholics, Protestants and Quakers, including George Fox and Mary Fell, have been imprisoned here for their beliefs. Amongst those taken to the moor for execution are the Lancashire witches of Pendle.

Up to the Bankruptcy Act of 1869 the Norman keep was used as a debtors' prison and even today part of the castle is used as a prison.

A guided tour is available for parts of the castle and includes the Shire Hall (1796–8) which is now used for civil cases at the assizes. There is a superb collection of shields bearing coats of arms said to be the finest in England. The crown court, jury rooms and library can also be seen if the courts are not in session. Other highlights include the castle museum in Hadrian's Tower with its instruments of torture and punishment, the drop room where prisoners were pinioned before being taken for execution, and a visit to the dungeons.

*The castle is open from Good Friday to the end of September from 10.30am to 4.00pm when courts are not in session. A charge is made but taking photographs is prohibited. Telephone (0524) 64998. Near to the castle is the Judge's Lodgings Museum.*

*St Mary's Priory.*

## The Judge's Lodgings Museum

THIS seventeenth-century house is now used as a museum of Lancashire childhood and also holds a collection of Gillow furniture set in period rooms.

*The Museum is open from Good Friday to the end of October. Telephone (0524) 32808.*

*Downhill from the museum and across King Street lies an old-fashioned coffee and tea shop, which is recommended. To reach the Market Square and City Museum, cross King Street and take the first road to the right. The City Museum houses a collection of local life from early times to the present day together with the collection of the King's Own Regiment. Guided walks, from the third Wednesday in July to the third Wednesday in September, leave from the museum.*

## The Williamson Memorial

EASTWARD and outside the town centre is Ashton Park and the landmark Williamson Memorial. This thirty-eight acre park is crowned by the folly commissioned by James Williamson, the first Lord Ashton. The building is a memorial to his family and was given to the people of Lancaster. The Williamsons were one of the two major linoleum manufacturers in the city.

Built of white Portland stone and designed in high baroque style by Sir John Belcher, the memorial now houses an exhibition of the life and work of the Williamson family and of their industrial rivals. There is an audio-visual presentation of Edwardian life and, from the high gallery, there are extensive views over the town, the Lancashire coastline, Morecambe Bay and the Lake District. The former orangery now houses a tropical butterfly house and, in summer, the park is taken over each evening for promenade presentations of Shakespearean and other appropriate theatrical productions.

*The Memorial building is open from the first of May until the end of September and also at Easter from 10.00 a.m. to 5.00 p.m.. During winter it is open from 12.00 noon to 4.00 p.m. but the butterfly house is closed from November to January. Admission is free to the park and memorial but not to the Edwardian presentation, the gallery or the butterfly house. Telephone (0524) 33318.*